STOIC
TEMPERANCE
10 sure lessons
to cultivate
calmness
ADRIAN WALTERS

I0695646

Copyright © 2023 by Adrian Walters

All rights reserved.

No part of this publication may be reproduced, distributed, or transmitted in any form or by any means, including photocopying, recording, or other electronic or mechanical methods, without the prior written permission of the publisher, except as permitted by U.S. copyright law.

Table Of Contents

Introduction

Temperance is the supreme mastery of consciously refusing rather than responding. It is the art of making deliberate choices as opposed to impulsive ones. Temperance is one of the four fundamental qualities, along with wisdom, justice, and courage, according to the Stoics. It entails exercising restraint and moderation, being aware of our limitations, and controlling our passions. It is the capacity to maintain composure in the face of difficulties and react in a thoughtful, proportionate manner. In a nutshell, temperance is the moderation that permeates all facets of life and is in a balanced state. This virtue is crucial because it affects our capacity to remain calm and rational under pressure, to make wise judgments, to efficiently solve difficulties. You may have a major problem with self-control if your emotions, whether they be anger or enthusiasm, frequently control you. Stoicism is one strategy we use to get over this obstacle.

I want to be straightforward and applicable in this book. I'll outline ten concrete examples of how to use the fundamental historical concepts to promote temperance as one of your virtues.

Lesson One

Avoid Being Led By Desires

True freedom comes from having control over your desires, not from having too many of them. According to the Stoics, our persistent desire for pleasure and fear of discomfort turn us into prisoners who are controlled by our impulses rather than by ourselves. Here, it's important to focus on long-term benefits rather than short-term pleasures while making judgments. Delaying gratification can be an excellent place to start.

As opposed to focusing on short-term rewards, it is helpful to set long-term goals and break them down into manageable chunks. Keep in mind that getting there is just as crucial as being there. If we apply this to any endeavor, a more fulfilling life will start to take shape.

Lesson Two

Continue Learning And Growing

Philosophy makes no promises to the outside world. Through continuous learning and personal development, stoicism is the path to achieving temperance. The way to virtue and knowledge, according to the stoics, is a lifelong adventure. We frequently make the error of starting along the path while considering the end point and reward when the path itself should be the prize.

You can apply this approach to your life by devoting time every day to learning something new or reflecting on your experiences and what you can gain from them. This can not only help you develop as a person but also provide you a wider perspective to deal with the difficulties of life with more equilibrium and serenity.

Lesson Three

Recognize And Appreciate What You

Have

Spend a moment each day acknowledging and appreciating what you have. Having a home to live, food on the table, and loved ones at your side can all be considered basic necessities. For this exercise, keeping a thankfulness notebook can be a useful tool. List three things for which you are grateful. You can also go for a walk in the outdoors every day and be mindful of your surroundings. Recognize that you already have enough to be happy and cultivate a mindset of satisfaction. Meditation on thankfulness can be a potent tool for developing appreciation in daily life.

Moving on from the last point, focus on being grateful and let go of the need for things to happen the way you want it to. Find satisfaction in the way things are and learn to accept situations as they arise. For the Stoics, gratitude is both a way of thinking and a way of living. It gives us the ability to concentrate on the good things rather than the bad. Remember to show your gratitude in concrete ways, such as by expressing "thank you" more frequently, sending handwritten letters to people who have gone above and beyond for you, or just pausing to take in the beauty of your surroundings. Keep a safe distance from someone who taints your thankfulness, in particular.

Avoid those who propagate unkind words and grievances. Respect what you already have because true wealth is found more in appreciating what you already have than in yearning for what you don't. Stoics emphasized simplicity and moderation by building thankfulness for what we already have rather than always craving more.

Lesson Four

Develop The Ability To Deal With Challenges

Seneca once said that it was hardships that awoke brilliance. We are reminded by historical teachings that challenges and failures are occasions for growth and learning. The best approach to apply this idea to your life is to develop resilience. This entails handling challenges with composure and equilibrium, seeing setbacks as opportunities for growth rather than as indications of personal failure. A part of this process also include learning how to solve problems and adopting a progressive mindset.

As you come to understand that you can grow and learn from your mistakes and difficulties, you should adopt a growth-oriented mentality to view obstacles as opportunities. Practice resilience by developing the abilities and methods that help you go through challenges in order to grow and learn.

Lesson Five

Live In The Present

Keep in mind that you don't see reality as it is; rather, you see it as you are. Stoicism emphasizes the importance of being in the now. Our fears of the future or our regrets about the past are the main sources of our worry and anxieties. We can rid ourselves from these worries and preserve peace and tranquility by concentrating on the present moment.

A useful strategy for applying this idea is to practice mindfulness. This can entail setting aside time each day to meditate or simply pay attention to the sensations of the moment while focusing on the present. Avoid multitasking and try to focus only on one task at a time to achieve this. Practice mindfulness through engaging in regular meditation or by being conscious of your daily activities and interactions with others.

Lesson Six

Practice Empathy

Everybody is facing their own difficulties, and the stoics remind us that life is an interpretation. By developing empathy, we may better comprehend people and react in a way that upholds harmony and peace.

Try to put yourself in others' shoes before passing judgment or responding to something to put this into practice. This might entail pausing to contemplate the viewpoint of another person before replying or actively looking for chances to discover perspectives and experiences that are different from your own.

By applying this approach and developing your empathy, you will progressively be able to understand different points of view without getting angry or reacting in a destructive way.

Lesson Seven

Accept What You Cannot Change

According to Epictetus, "It is not the facts that disturb men, but their judgment of the facts." This is a key component of stoicism that is emphasized repeatedly in my other publications. Living a peaceful existence will depend on the notion that we should accept the things we cannot alter and concentrate on the things we can.

There are many ways to put this theory into reality. Learning to distinguish between what we can influence through our actions and what is entirely out of our control is one of them. The weather serves as a very simple and straightforward example. Worrying about the weather is a pointless waste of energy because we can never predict whether it will be sunny or stormy. We can instead concentrate on how we would get ready for and react to various weather circumstances.

Cognitive therapy approaches that assist us in identifying and challenging unjustified or harmful thoughts are another way to put this notion into effect. We will be relieved of a significant source of concern and be able to live in a more calm and balanced manner once we learn to accept the things that we cannot alter.

Lesson Eight

Accept Your Strengths And Weaknesses

Recognize that you are flawed because you are a human. Watch how nature responds to and adjusts to change. You may be motivated to follow suit by this. Give your mental health a high priority and open out to dependable friends about your experiences and emotions. To overcome failures, start with basic measures and take baby steps. Adversities are a natural part of life; accept them and be gentle to yourself when they arise.

Lesson Nine

Practice Detachment

According to Epictetus, "poverty does not consist in the decrease of possessions, but in the increase of avarice." In the context of stoicism, detachment refers to letting go of an unhealthy reliance on other people or things to bring you satisfaction. It's not about shunning all pleasures or material possessions, but rather about not letting them be the exclusive source of your inner calm.

Detachment can be practiced in many different ways. One method can be meditation, when you visualize your wants and then see letting them go. Another method is to simplify your life, acquire fewer things, and put more emphasis on people and experiences rather than material stuff because we frequently have more than we need or deserve.

By placing a high value on simplicity and moderation, we free ourselves from the constant search for novelty and advancement.

Lesson Ten

Self-care

This is the final but most important step. In order for the mind to remain strong and healthy, you must first keep your body in good shape. Stoicism recognizes the interdependence of the body and mind operating as one. One of the most important aspects of developing temperance is maintaining a healthy body.

It comprises taking care of your physical health, which includes working out frequently, eating a nutritious diet, and getting enough sleep, as well as your mental health, whether through meditation treatment or just making time for relaxation and activities you genuinely like. Keep in mind that failing to take good care of your physical appearance and health is disrespectful. Find a hobby you actually like, and make a commitment to practicing it frequently.

Conclusion

Tradition has claimed that temperance leads to inner calm and tranquility. In contrast to letting our emotions and impulses rule us, it focuses on helping us understand and manage them. We learn to live by our beliefs and respond to life's problems rather than reacting by practicing temperance.

According to Marcus Aurelius, "The happiness of your life depends on the quality of your thoughts." Frequently, what we constantly believe becomes our reality.

www.ingramcontent.com/pod-product-compliance
Lightning Source LLC
Chambersburg PA
CBHW071051260726

48660CB00008B/3163